MEEKNESS

A DIVINE PATH TO EXALTATION

JOSHUA ASIEDU

EPIGNOSIS
PUBLISHING
HOUSE

-epignosis-

MEEKNESS: A Divine Path To Exaltation

Copyright © 2025 by Joshua Asiedu.

For information contact :

(jkasiedu1@gmail.com)

First Edition: November 2025

BOOK AND COVER BY PJOSH DESIGNS

ISBN **979-8-9938958-0-2**

CONTENTS

CHAPTER ONE

Do Not Exalt Yourself

WE ARE EMBARKING ON A JOURNEY to manifest a powerful virtue from the fruit of the Spirit: meekness. Specifically, we will be looking at the vital command, "Exalt not thyself." In our modern culture, especially here in the West, meekness is profoundly misunderstood. It is rarely considered a virtue; more often, it is mistaken for weakness, seen as being timid, passive, or easily pushed around. But I want to assure you that nothing could be further from the truth.

The core of our message is this: meekness is a mighty virtue for every believer. It is an indispensable quality for anyone who truly wants to go up in God. Why? Because when God is choosing those He will appoint to the top, He consistently looks for and chooses from this specific category of people: the meek ones. So, I invite you to set aside the world's flawed definitions and join me. Let us move beyond cultural misconceptions to explore the true biblical meaning of meekness and discover the divine power that unlocks God's promotion in our lives.

Biblical Meekness Defined

To truly embrace meekness, we must first build our understanding not on human opinion but on the unchanging truth of Scripture. The world may offer its definitions, but they fall short of the rich and powerful picture painted in the Bible. To grasp what God means when He calls us to be meek, we must look at the concepts and examples He Himself has given us. We will look at the three facets of Meekness.

Meekness as Spiritual "Poverty"

One of the most profound ways the Bible describes meekness is through the concept of being "poor." Now, this isn't referring to someone who lacks material possessions. It describes a state of the heart— a state of total dependence on God.

We see this connection clearly when we compare a prophecy in Isaiah with its fulfillment in the words of Jesus. In Isaiah, the prophet foretells the Messiah's mission:

The Spirit of the Lord God is upon me; because the Lord hath anointed me to preach good tidings unto the meek; he hath sent me to bind up the brokenhearted, to proclaim liberty to the captives, and the opening of the prison to them that are bound

— **Isaiah 61:1 (KJV)**

Centuries later, when Jesus stood up in the synagogue and read from this very scroll, He quoted the passage this way:

"The Spirit of the Lord is upon me, because he hath anointed me to preach the gospel to the poor; he hath sent me to heal the brokenhearted, to preach deliverance to the captives, and recovering of sight to the blind, to set at liberty them that are bruised."

— **Luke 4:18 (KJV)**

Notice the direct parallel: where Isaiah used the word *meek*, Jesus used the word *poor*. This was a divine clarification. This "poverty" is a spiritual state. King David, a man of immense wealth and power, understood this perfectly. In one of his psalms, he wrote: *"This poor man cried, and the LORD heard him, and saved him out of all his troubles."*

— **Psalm 34:6 (KJV)**

David wasn't lacking for anything financially, but he called himself a "poor man" because he recognized his utter dependence on God. This spiritual "poverty" is the deep, internal acknowledgment that we can do nothing of true spiritual value on our own; we need God for everything. Jesus Himself modeled this complete dependence, stating plainly:

...Verily, verily, I say unto you, The Son can do nothing of himself, but what he seeth the Father do: for what things soever he doeth, these also doeth the Son likewise. — **John 5:19 (KJV)**

And He taught us that the same principle applies to us: "I am the vine, ye are the branches: He that *abideth in me, and I in him, the same bringeth forth much fruit: for without me ye can do nothing"* **(John 15:5).** This is the heart of meekness: a humble recognition that without Christ, we can accomplish nothing of eternal worth.

Meekness as Humility

The second facet of meekness is humility and a lowly heart. There is no greater example of this than Jesus Christ. He described Himself with these very words:

Take my yoke upon you, and learn of me; for I am meek and lowly in heart: and ye shall find rest for your souls — **Matthew 11:29 (KJV)**

The New Living Translation renders "meek and lowly" as "humble and gentle." Jesus, the Son of God, declared, "I am humble." If Jesus Himself is humble, why are we so often proud? Meekness is not just an outward posture; it is an inward state of humility.

I'm reminded of a story about a young boy whose teacher sternly told him, "You must sit down!" The boy physically sat, but with a defiant spirit. He looked up at her and declared, "Although I'm sitting here physically, in my heart I'm standing up!" Many of us can be like that boy. We can put on an outward show of humility, but inside, our hearts are standing tall with pride. True meekness, the kind Jesus models, is a genuine humility that starts from within.

Meekness as Being Small in Your Own Eyes

Finally, this state of dependence and humility finds its outward expression in being "small in your own eyes." This quality is what allowed King David to worship God with an abandon that others found scandalous.

When the Ark of the Lord was finally being brought into Jerusalem, David was overcome with joy. The Bible says he "danced before the LORD with all his might," casting off his royal robes to celebrate freely. He was coming home with great joy, ready to bless his family after this momentous occasion. But when he arrived, his wife Michal, the daughter of the former king, Saul, met him at the door and destroyed his happiness. She was appalled, mocking him for uncovering himself and dancing shamelessly before the servant girls.

Michal was used to the dignified royalty of her father. Saul would never have danced like that; he was the type to march in with his regalia after the praise was over, demanding that everyone stand. But David was not like that. He was willing to be undignified, to play and be joyful before his God. His response to her critique is a masterclass in meekness:

And David said unto Michal, It was before the LORD, which chose me before thy father, and before all his house, to appoint me ruler over the people of the LORD, over Israel: therefore will I play before the LORD. And I will yet be more vile than thus, and will be base in mine own sight: and of the maidservants which thou hast spoken of, of them shall I be had in honour. — **2 Samuel 6:21-22 (KJV)**

David's words are astonishing. He essentially said, "You think this is undignified? I'm just getting started. I will be even more base, more *small in my own sight*." This is the fruit of biblical meekness. Because David knew he was utterly dependent on the God who had chosen him, he refused to see himself as a big, important king in His presence. The story ends with a sobering consequence for Michal's pride. Because she looked down on David's humble worship, the Bible records that she "had no child unto the day of her death" (**2 Samuel 6:23**).

These three facets—dependence on God, a humble heart, and being small in our own eyes—form the biblical foundation of meekness. They reveal a spirit that receives God's exaltation. But this spirit stands in direct opposition to its lethal counterfeit, the pride that leads us down the perilous path of self-exaltation.

The Peril of Pride: Exalt Not Thyself

Understanding the danger of pride is a matter of spiritual life and death. Self-exaltation is not a simple character flaw; it is a spiritually lethal path that leads directly to what the Bible calls "the condemnation of the devil." Once a person is promoted, they become a target for this temptation. Some become so lifted up that, as I like to say, even God needs to follow protocol to be able to talk to them. To avoid this fate, we must understand the origin of pride and recognize its destructive pattern.

The Origin of Pride

The very first being to fall was brought down by pride. The Apostle Paul warns that a leader in the church must not be a novice, lest he repeat this tragic history:

Lest being lifted up with pride he fall into the condemnation of the devil. — **1 Timothy 3:6 (KJV)**

The condemnation of the devil *is* pride. To understand his fall, we turn to the prophet Isaiah, who records the inner monologue of Lucifer:

How art thou fallen from heaven, O Lucifer, son of the morning! how art thou cut down to the ground, which didst weaken the nations! For thou hast said in thine heart, I will ascend into heaven, I will exalt my throne above the stars of God: I will sit also upon the mount of the congregation, in the sides of the north: I will ascend above the heights of the clouds; I will be like the most High. Yet thou shalt be brought down to hell, to the sides of the pit. — **Isaiah 14:12-15 (KJV)**

Knowing what brought him down, Satan uses this same temptation against humanity. When he came to Adam and Eve, he whispered the same lie, inviting them to exalt themselves:

For God doth know that in the day ye eat thereof, then your eyes shall be opened, and ye shall be as gods, knowing good and evil. — **Genesis 3:5 (KJV)**

The Contrast: Christ's Humility

Against the dark backdrop of Satan's pride stands the brilliant light of Christ's humility. Where Satan's five arrogant "I will's" led to his downfall, Christ's five humble actions led to His ultimate exaltation.

"Let this mind be in you, which was also in Christ Jesus: Who, being in the form of God, thought it not robbery to be equal with God: But made himself of no reputation, and took upon him the form of a servant, and was made in the likeness of men: And being found in fashion as a man, he humbled himself, and became obedient unto death, even the death of the cross."
– **Philippians 2:5-8 (KJV)**

This is the mind God wants us to have: *"Let this mind be in you, which was also in Christ Jesus"* (Phili 2:5). Let us contrast their paths directly:

- Satan declared, **"I will ascend… I will be like the most High,"** grasping for a position that was not his. But Jesus, "Who, being in the form of God, **thought it not robbery to be equal with God.**" He refused to grasp what was rightfully His.

- Satan proclaimed, **"I will exalt my throne."** But Jesus **"made himself of no reputation."**

- Satan boasted, **"I will sit also upon the mount of the congregation."** But Jesus **"took upon him the form of a servant."**

- Satan said in his heart, **"I will ascend above the heights of the clouds."** But Jesus **"humbled himself."**

- Satan sought ultimate power and authority. But Jesus **"became obedient unto death, even the death of the cross."**

And what was the result of this profound self-humbling? The scripture declares, *"Wherefore God also hath highly exalted him, and given him a name which is above every name"* (**Philippians 2:9**). But of Satan the scripture states, "*Yet thou shalt be brought down to hell, to the sides of the pit*" **(Isaiah 14:15).** God is not against you being exalted. He is against you trying to lift yourself up.

A Spiritual Law: The Way Up is Down

This contrast reveals a universal spiritual law: the way up is down. Jesus stated this principle plainly: *And whosoever shall exalt himself shall be abased; and he that shall humble himself shall be exalted.*

— **Matthew 23:12 (KJV)**

This is a spiritual certainty. It also reveals a critical distinction we must understand. Notice that you are the one who is to humble yourself. It is our job. When God has to humble you, it is because you have already exalted yourself. That is not humility; it is humiliation.

Jesus illustrated this with a practical parable at a banquet, where he saw guests rushing to the best seats. He used this moment to teach:

When someone invites you to a wedding feast, do not take the place of honor, for a person more distingui-shed than you may have been invited. If so, the host who invited both of you will come and say to you, 'Give this person your seat.' Then, humiliated, you will have to take the least important place. But when you are invited, take the lowest place, so that when your host comes, he will say to you, 'Friend, move up to a better place.' Then you will be honored in the presence of all the other guests. — **Luke 14:8-10 (NIV)**

Imagine the shame of being asked to move down, versus the honor of being publicly invited to move up. I experienced this myself once. As a very young officiating minister, I went to a wedding at a large church. When I arrived, the usher looked at me—young and without a wedding ring—and hesitated to take me to the platform where the other ministers were. Instead, he directed me to a seat in the congregation. Rather than make a fuss, I found a way to serve. Seeing they needed a bassist, I went up and began to play. Much later, someone informed the senior pastor that I was one of the officiating ministers. He called for me from the platform. By then, every other seat was filled except for one—right beside him, in the place of highest honor. I walked up majestically, sat down, and was later asked to lead a major prayer.

This principle is unwavering. If you make it your job to humble yourself, God will make it His job to lift you up. This is the universal law of His kingdom, a law that one tragic king forgot, leading to his own destruction.

A Cautionary Tale

The life of King Uzziah serves as one of the most sobering warnings in all of Scripture. His story teaches us that the need for meekness does not diminish with success; on the contrary, it becomes more critical than ever. He began well, but his end is a cautionary tale about what happens when God-given strength is poisoned by a prideful heart.

The Rise of a King

Uzziah's reign started with great promise. He was a righteous king, and the Bible gives us the key to his early success:

And he sought God in the days of Zechariah, who had understanding in the visions of God: and as long as he sought the Lord, God made him to prosper.

— 2 Chron. 26:5 (KJV)

And prosper he did. He won military victories, strengthened his kingdom, and even became an inventor of war machines. His fame spread far and wide. The scripture summarizes his incredible rise with a crucial phrase:

...for he was marvellously helped, till he was strong.

— 2 Chronicles 26:15 (KJV)

God helped him on every level. But that very strength, which was a gift from God, became a dangerous trap.

The Fall from Grace

The moment of his turn is stated with tragic clarity. The help he received made him strong, and that strength led to his downfall.

But when he was strong, his heart was lifted up to his destruction: for he transgressed against the LORD his God, and went into the temple of the LORD to burn incense upon the altar of incense.

— 2 Chronicles 26:16 (KJV)

This was a serious transgression. The duty of burning incense was reserved exclusively for the consecrated priests. Uzziah, filled with pride from his many successes, felt he was now on such good terms with God that he could disregard the rules. He walked into the temple, intending to take on a role that was not his.

The priests bravely confronted him, but Uzziah became enraged. As he stood there, holding the censer, divine judgment struck instantly. While he was filled with wrath toward the priests, leprosy rose up on his forehead, right there in the temple beside the incense altar. The consequence was immediate, public, and permanent. The humiliation was so complete that the king who had boldly entered God's house to usurp a holy office was now in a panicked hurry to flee from it. He *"himself hasted also to go out, because the LORD had smitten him"* (**2 Chron. 26:20**).

Uzziah's story drives home the lesson with terrifying clarity: the strength, success, and help that God gives us become a deadly trap the moment they breed pride in our hearts. He exalted himself, and God brought him low.

Choose Your Path

As we conclude this chapter, the message is clear and the choice is stark. We all stand at a crossroads, faced with two distinct paths. One is the path of Lucifer and Uzziah—the path of self-exaltation. It promises power, recognition, and control, but it always ends in being brought low. The other is the path of David and, supremely, of Jesus Christ—the path of humility. It requires us to become dependent, to embrace a lowly heart, and to remain small in our own eyes.

I want to make a direct, pastoral appeal to you. Make it your life's work to humble yourself. Do not seek position; seek submission. No matter what successes you achieve, no matter how much God marvelously helps you, determine in your heart to stay small in your own sight. As soon as you approach the gate of His presence, drop your titles. You are coming before the One who gave you the title in the first place.

CHAPTER TWO

Under The Mighty Hand Of God

IN THE PREVIOUS CHAPTER, WE BEGAN TO explore the profound strength found in meekness. Now, I want to build upon that foundation by examining one of the most practical and powerful instructions in all of Scripture. Our guide for this journey is found in the first epistle of Peter, specifically chapter 5, verses 5 and 6. For years, believers have read these words, but I find that we often miss the depth of their meaning. We will therefore seek to answer a central question: What does it truly mean to humble ourselves "under the mighty hand of God"?

My conviction is that understanding this concept—not as a vague spiritual feeling, but as a series of concrete, daily actions—is the key to unlocking the divine promotion that God has promised for each of our lives. It is the pathway to the exaltation He has prepared for us, and it is a path we must choose to walk.

Humility Before Exaltation

Before we can rise to the places God has for us, it is important that we understand His timing and His methods. The desire for significance, for prominence, and for a return to the glory God originally intended for humanity is a legitimate, God-given longing. We were made for more. However, God's pathway to that "more" is entirely counterintuitive to the world's approach of self-promotion and relentless striving. In God's kingdom, there is an unshakable principle: humility always comes before exaltation.

The Call to Humility

The Apostle Peter lays out this divine protocol with perfect clarity. The responsibility for this first step is placed squarely on our shoulders.
"Humble yourselves therefore under the mighty hand of God, that he may exalt you in due time:"
— **1 Peter 5:6 (KJV)**

Notice the active command: "Humble *yourselves*." This is not something we can delegate to God in prayer. We cannot ask, "God, come and humble me." He has given the instruction to us. It is our prerogative, our choice, and our responsibility to walk in humility. If I am not humble, the fault lies with me and no one else. This personal act of humbling is the non-negotiable prerequisite for God's act of exalting.

One of the greatest obstacles to God's divine order is our own human nature, particularly the ambition and impatience that so often characterize the young. A young person, full of energy and vision, sees someone who has achieved success—the nice house, the accolades, the influence—and wants to get there tomorrow. This mindset often leads to intense but short-lived spiritual efforts, like a week of dry fasting, followed by frustration when the doors of opportunity don't immediately swing open.

Youthful haste doesn't understand the wisdom of process. It fails to grasp the critical phrase in Peter's instruction: "in due time." God has a "due time" for your promotion, and rushing ahead of His schedule only leads to disappointment.

The Law of Pride and humility

The choice before us is stark, and the consequences are absolute. Pride and humility set us on two completely different trajectories. To walk in pride is to set yourself on a course for a direct collision with God. And here is a profound truth we often miss: when we are proud, God Himself becomes the stumbling block in our path. You may think Satan is the one stopping you. You may be praying and fasting for God to remove the obstacle, but all the while, God *is* the stumbling block because of your pride.

In contrast, humility positions us to receive His unmerited favor. The principle is as simple as it is profound: if we exalt ourselves, we will inevitably be brought down. But if we choose to humble ourselves, God Himself will exalt us. Peter states this law of the Spirit plainly:

Likewise, ye younger, submit yourselves unto the elder. Yea, all of you be subject one to another, and be clothed with humility: for God resisteth the proud, and giveth grace to the humble. — **1 Peter 5:5 (KJV)**

This brings us back to the central command. We are to humble ourselves not in a vacuum, but in a very specific place: "under the mighty hand of God." To walk this path, we must first correctly define our location.

Submission to God's Authority

When Scripture uses metaphorical language, it is essential that we seek its intended meaning. The phrase "the mighty hand of God" is not an invitation to find a literal, physical hand to kneel beneath. It is a powerful biblical term that represents a specific and tangible concept in the life of every believer. If we misinterpret the location, we will fail to practice the command.

The prophet Jeremiah provides a perfect key to unlocking this metaphor. In Jeremiah chapter 27, God gives him a message for the surrounding kings, declaring His supreme sovereignty over all their lands. *"I have made the earth, the man and the beast that are upon the ground, by my great power and by my outstretched arm, and have given it unto whom it seemed meet unto me. And now have I given all these lands into the hand of Nebuchadnezzar the king of Babylon, my servant; and the beasts of the field have I given him also to serve him."* — **Jer. 27:5-6 (KJV)**

God states that He has placed these nations "into the hand of" a foreign, pagan king. What does this mean in practical terms? The Holman Christian Standard Bible (HCSB) translation clarifies the phrase perfectly, rendering it as: "I have placed all these lands **under the authority** of My servant Nebuchad-nezzar."

Herein is our definition: To be "in the hand of" someone is to be under the authority of that person. Therefore, biblically, "under the mighty hand of God" is a direct command to place ourselves under the authority of God.

The Scope of God's Authority in Christ

So, where is God's authority found? The custodian of all of God's authority in this age is the Lord Jesus Christ. After His resurrection, Jesus made a declaration of breathtaking scope:

And Jesus came and spake unto them, saying, All power is given unto me in heaven and in earth.

— **Matthew 28:18 (KJV)**

The word for "power" here is *exousia*, which means authority. All authority—not some, but all—in both the heavenly and earthly realms has been given to Jesus. This means that every legitimate structure of authority on earth, whether it is governmental, institutional, or in the home, is an extension of the authority of Jesus Christ Himself. To submit to these authorities is to submit to the one who holds all authority.

The One Forbidden Authority

There is only one sphere of authority that a believer is strictly forbidden to submit to: the authority of darkness. This authority manifests in false religions, cults, and practices like witchcraft. The Apostle Paul makes it clear that this is a domain from which we have been permanently removed. In Colossians 1:13, he writes that God "has rescued us from the domain of darkness and transferred us into the kingdom of the Son He loves" (HCSB).

We should not fear this authority. I have heard stories that illustrate our misplaced fear. One man, tired of people urinating on his fence, put up signs threatening fines, but nothing worked. Finally, he posted a new sign: "We need pee for ritual sacrifice." The problem stopped immediately. In another instance a man in a dispute threatened his opponent, "I'm going to take you to my lawyer!" The other man replied, "I'll take you to my herbalist." The first man immediately backed down. You see, we fear those things even more than God. That's the actual thing God says we should not be afraid of; that's the one we are afraid of. We are not under that authority, and we must never submit to it.

Having defined God's authority and its one exception, we can now turn to the practical, everyday spheres where God commands us to walk in submission.

Honoring God's Delegated Authorities

True submission to God is not a hidden, internal feeling or a mystical state of being. It is a visible, practical, and daily demonstration of our respect for His authority. The Bible asks a piercing question: "How can you love a God you cannot see, but not the brother you can see?" Scripture calls that "fake love." By the same logic, how can you claim to humbly submit to God's unseen authority while actively disrespecting, dishonoring, and resisting the authorities He has placed right in front of you? That is what I call "fake submission." Humbling ourselves under God's mighty hand means submitting to His delegated authorities.

Sphere 1: Submission to Government

The highest earthly authority God has established is civil government. A true Christian is a good citizen. The Bible is unequivocal on this point.

- **1 Peter 2:13-14** commands us to "*Submit yourselves to every ordinance of man for the*

Lord's sake: whether it be to the king, as supreme; Or unto governors..."

- **Titus 3:1** instructs believers to be "*subject to principalities and powers, to obey magistrates.*" This includes everyday laws, such as obeying traffic lights.

- **Romans 13:1-4** explains that "the powers that be are ordained of God" and that whoever "*resisteth the power, resisteth the ordinance of God: and they that resist shall receive to themselves damnation,*" or destruction. The ruler is called "the minister of God."

This principle is so absolute that God punished His own people for violating it. In Jeremiah 27:8-11, God declared He would punish Judah for refusing to submit to the king of Babylon. What makes this so staggering is that God was commanding submission to Nebuchadnezzar—a very terrible idol worshipper— whom God Himself designated as "my servant" because he occupied a seat of God-ordained authority. Their refusal to submit brought destruction upon them

Sphere 2: Submission to Employers

In the workplace, the authority of an employer is a legitimate, God-ordained authority that we must honor. **Ephesians 6:5-8** instructs, *"Servants, be obedient to them that are your masters according to the flesh, with fear and trembling, in singleness of your heart, as unto Christ."* This work is not to be done with "eye service," only performing when the boss is watching, but *"as the servants of Christ, doing the will of God from the heart."*

Our first and most effective sermon in the workplace is the excellence of our work. When Joseph was a slave in Potiphar's house, his master, who did not know God, saw that the Lord was with Joseph because everything he touched prospered. A believer's first act of witness is to do an excellent job. It is not our place to use work time for inappropriate preaching; you are called there to work. If you do, you are the one out of line. Our first preaching is to give them good service, thereby honoring God and the authority He has placed over us.

Sphere 3: Submission to Husbands

Within the covenant of marriage, God has established an order of authority for the health and stability of the family. Paul said, *"Wives, submit yourselves unto your own husbands, as unto the Lord. For the husband is the head of the wife, even as Christ is the head of the church... Therefore as the church is subject unto Christ, so let the wives be to their own husbands in everything."* —**Ephesians 5:22-24** (KJV)

This command is directed to a wife concerning her "own husband" and is to be done "as unto the Lord," recognizing it as an act of obedience to God's design. This is a matter of accepting God-ordained structure, not an indication of superiority or inferiority. Just as the church can never be the head of Christ, so the divine order in the home is set.

Sphere 4: Submission of Children to Parents

God commands children to submit to the authority of their parents, attaching a unique blessing to this instruction. **Ephesians 6:1-3** says, *"Children, obey your parents in the Lord: for this is right. Honour thy father and mother; which is the first commandment with promise; That it may be well with thee, and thou mayest live long on the earth."*

Your parents have gone to work, crashing their heads to put food on the table. They stayed up through sleepless nights when you were sick. And you don't want to listen to them? But your friend that has not bought even a candy for you, he has not bought even chips for you—that one's voice is the one you like. It is a dangerous trade. Even Jesus, the Son of God, "was subject to his parents" during his childhood, as recorded in the Gospel of Luke.

Sphere 5: Submission to Church Elders

Within the local church, God has appointed elders and pastors to provide spiritual oversight, and members are commanded to submit to their leadership.

Hebrews 13:17 instructs, "*Obey them that have the rule over you, and submit yourselves: for they watch for your souls, as they that must give account, that they may do it with joy, and not with grief: for that is unprofitable for you.*"

Making a pastor's job difficult through resistance or strife is, according to Scripture, "unprofitable" for the one causing the grief. A believer who causes their pastor to lead with a squeezed face and a heavy heart will find that they cannot be prayed for effectively. The blessing is cut off.

But when a congregation makes it possible for their leaders to serve with joy, it is profitable for everyone. For instance in our local congregation, When I kneel down to pray and I remember Sister Jenny, I can pray, "Oh God, what a great lady, thank you for her life and commitment!" When I remember Pastor Fred and his family, I think of his fervency in prayers, and I say, "Oh my goodness, Father, thank you!" When I think of the choir, who work so hard and double up in cleaning the church, I can pray, "Father, what a great choir bless them immensely!" When a pastor can do their job with joy, good things will be flowing.

Sphere 6: Submission to One Another

Finally, Scripture broadens the scope of submission to include our relationships with fellow believers. **Ephesians 5:21** calls us to be *submit ourselves "one to another in the fear of God."* **1 Peter 5:5** echoes the same: *"Yea, all of you be subject one to another, and be clothed with humility."* This means recognizing and respecting *situational authority* —honoring the person God has placed in charge of a specific area, at a specific time, out of reverence for Christ's ultimate authority. For example, our media director is the authority in the media department, while the youth leader is the authority in the youth meeting. A person must recognize who is in charge in a given situation and honor that structure.

Although I am the Pastor of our church, when I attend a men's fellowship meeting, I don't try to override their president's authority. Although I appointed him there, I submit myself to his authority at that point. For example, our men's president is also part of the media team, therefore, he summits himself to the media director during their operations and likewise, the media director summits himself to the men's president in the men's department. This is called mutual submission. We must recognize everyone's area of expertise and authority and honor them.

Conclusion: The Path to Your "Due Time"

The path to manifesting meekness is not found in a mystical feeling but in a series of clear, concrete, and daily choices. To humble ourselves under the mighty hand of God is to willingly and joyfully submit to the spheres of authority that He has sovereignly placed over us: in our nation, in our workplace, in our homes, in our church, and among our brothers and sisters in Christ.

This is true Christianity in practice. It is the visible evidence of a heart that trusts God's process. I can assure you that any person who chooses to walk this path of practical, daily submission is positioning themselves perfectly for the exaltation that is to come. For when we humble ourselves under His authority, we can be absolutely certain that He will lift us up in His perfect time.

CHAPTER THREE

Condescending To Men Of Low Estate

IN OUR LAST DISCUSSION, WE EXPLORED the vital importance of humility as it relates to submitting to the authorities God has placed over us—what the scripture calls humbling ourselves "under the mighty hand of God." We learned that our submission to government, employers, and church leaders is, in fact, an acknowledgment of the ultimate authority of Jesus Christ. This is one side of the coin of meekness, a crucial virtue for every believer.

However, there is another side to that coin, and I believe it presents an even greater test of a truly meek spirit. While submitting to those above us tests our obedience, how we treat those "below" us reveals the very core of our character. True humility isn't measured by how we bow to authority, but by how willingly we kneel to serve the overlooked. This is the heart of our study in this chapter as we deconstruct the powerful command found in Romans 12:16, which instructs us to *"Be of the same mind one toward another. Mind not high things, but **condescend to men of low estate.** Be not wise in your own conceits."*

This chapter will unpack what it means to overcome our natural, worldly tendencies and embrace this cornerstone of genuine, Christ-like humility. But first, we must understand the worldly system that this command so directly opposes.

The World's System vs. God's Command

To fully grasp the radical nature of God's command to "condescend," you must first understand the social structures of the world. Society naturally stratifies people, dividing them into different classes based on worldly measures of success and status. Social scientists often agree that these divisions are based on three primary criteria: a person's **occupation**, their **income**, and their level of **educational attainment**. Based on a 2005 analysis, this stratification often looks something like this:

- **The Upper Class:** This includes CEOs of major companies, celebrities, elite politicians, and those earning $200,000 or more annually.
- **The Upper Middle Class:** These are typically professionals with graduate degrees (doctorates, etc.), earning between $72,500 and $100,000 per year.
- **The Lower Middle Class:** This group consists of those with bachelor's degrees, often in professional support or sales roles, earning between $32,000 and $50,000.
- **The Working Class:** This includes individuals with diplomas or associate's degrees in clerical, service, or blue-collar jobs, with an annual income ranging from $15,000 to $25,000.
- **The Lower Class:** These are often part-time workers or the unemployed, possessing a high school diploma and earning $7,000 or less per year.

(Sources: Thompson & Hickey, Society in Focus, 2005
US Census Bureau Personal income and education of Individuals 25+, 2005)

As you walk through life, the world is constantly evaluating you—where you live, the job you do, the money you make—and placing you into one of these categories. But in the house of God, these divisions are explicitly forbidden. God does not see us through the world's lens. James warns the church against adopting this worldly system of honoring people based on their class.

He begins with a direct prohibition: *"My brethren, have not the faith of our Lord Jesus Christ, the Lord of glory, with respect of persons"* **(James 2:1).** James then provides a practical example of this sin in action:

For if there come unto your assembly a man with a gold ring, in goodly apparel, and there come in also a poor man in vile raiment; And ye have respect to him that weareth the gay clothing, and say unto him, Sit thou here in a good place; and say to the poor, Stand thou there, or sit here under my footstool: Are ye not then partial in yourselves, and are become judges of evil thoughts? — **James 2:2-4 (KJV)**

To have "respect of persons" is to treat people differently based on their wealth and appearance. James condemns this behavior as being "partial" and driven by "evil thoughts." It is a practice completely incompatible with faith in Jesus Christ. He continues by reminding us of God's perspective:

Hearken, my beloved brethren, Hath not God chosen the poor of this world rich in faith, and heirs of the kingdom which he hath promised to them that love him? But ye have despised the poor. Do not rich men oppress you, and draw you before the judgment seats? — **James 2:5-6 (KJV)**

It is critical, however, to distinguish this sin from the biblical command to honor those in authority. The Bible never commands us to honor people for their wealth or social status. It does, however, command us to honor the God-given positions they hold. For example, when our church district leader visits, we give him honor because of the authority he operates in, not because of any personal wealth. This is giving "honor to whom honor is due" (Romans 13:7). The sin of "respect of persons" occurs when you treat someone as special simply because they are wealthy or influential, while dismissing someone else who lacks those worldly advantages.

This sin of showing partiality, which James condemns as being driven by "evil thoughts," doesn't arise from a vacuum. It is rooted in two specific mindsets that the Apostle Paul commands us to overcome in our key text.

The First Prohibition: "Mind Not High Things"

The first great obstacle to developing a meek spirit is the sin of being highminded. This is a spiritual danger that causes us to fixate on status, prestige, and association with the elite. The Apostle Paul commands us directly, *"Mind not high things."* This is a call to resist the natural human tendency to be drawn only to what the world considers grand and important.

To be highminded is to be haughty—that is, bluntantly and disdainfully proud. It means having or showing an attitude of superiority and contempt for people or things perceived to be inferior. It is a characteristic that the Bible warns will define the perilous times of the last days:

*Charge them that are rich in this world, that they be not **highminded**, nor trust in uncertain riches, but in the living God, who giveth us richly all things to enjoy.* — **1 Timothy 6:17 (KJV)**

This know also, that in the last days perilous times shall come. For men shall be lovers of their own selves, covetous, boasters, proud, blasphemers, disobedient to parents, unthankful, unholy, Without natural affection, trucebreakers, false accusers, incontinent, fierce, despisers of those that are good, Traitors, heady, **highminded***, lovers of pleasures more than lovers of God;* — **2 Timothy 3:1-4 (KJV)**

The fact that "highminded" is on this list reveals just how serious it is in God's eyes. It is not a minor flaw but a defining feature of a world turning away from Him. May God deliver us. In practice, this attitude can manifest in many ways:

- **Carrying an air of importance** and expecting preferential treatment. You might recognize the rich man in a comedy sketch who, unwilling to wait in a long bank line, shouted, "I'm closing my account!" just to get the manager's immediate attention.

- **Associating only with the elite**, chasing celebrities for selfies to post on social media to build up your own image, as if a two-second encounter implies a deep relationship.

- **Living beyond your means to impress others.** Think of buying expensive designer clothes or thousand dollar Brazilian hair on a

$500-a-week income, all to impress people who, frankly, do not care.

- **Being ashamed of your own family**, like a young person at school who is embarrassed when their working-class father comes to visit because he doesn't fit the high-class image they are trying to project.

- **Pretending to be wealthy when you are not.** It's like a joke I heard of a man, back home during Christmas, who had no food. To keep up appearances, he would heat red oil until it was scorching and then drop in droplets of water. The sizzling sound and the smell mimicked frying chicken, so he could stand at his door with a toothpick, giving everyone the impression he had eaten well.

The Bible speaks directly to this kind of pretense. *"He that is despised, and hath a servant, is better than he that honoureth himself, and lacketh bread."* — **Proverbs 12:9 (KJV)**

Another scripture here says,

"There is he that maketh himself rich, yet hath nothing, and there is he that maketh himself poor, yet hath great riches." —**Proverbs 13:7 (KJV)**

Let us never pretend to be in a class where we do not belong. Our true worth comes not from our possessions or our status, but from the precious blood of Jesus that was shed for us. All the glories of this world are as fleeting as the "flower of grass." Resisting the urge to "mind high things" is the first step, but it must be paired with overcoming an internal arrogance.

The Second Prohibition: "Be Not Wise in Your Own Conceits"

While minding high things is about our outward associations and status, the second prohibition—*"Be not wise in your own conceits"*—deals with an internal dimension of pride. This is the arrogance that convinces us we are smarter than everyone else, that our opinions are superior, and that our contributions are always the most valuable. It is an intellectual pride that looks down on others.

Different translations help clarify this command: "Don't overestimate yourself," "Don't be proud and feel that you are smarter than others," or "Don't become set in your own opinions." Have you ever met people who are wise in their own conceits? They are often very opinionated. They feel the need to add their "two cents" to every discussion, embellishing what others have said to make it seem complete only after their input. They can become what I call a "local champion"—someone who thrives in an environment where their opinion is always seen as the best, but who cannot handle being in a place where other, more insightful contributions are made. This attitude can stem from educational attainment, causing someone with a master's degree to look down on the insights of someone who attended a "local government community school."

This worldly "wisdom" that puffs up is the complete opposite of the wisdom that comes from God. The book of James draws a sharp contrast between the two. First, he describes the mark of true, godly wisdom: *Who is a wise man and endued with knowledge among you? let him shew out of a good conversation his works with meekness of wisdom.*
— **James 3:13 (KJV)**

The defining characteristic of heavenly wisdom is **"meekness."** Any wisdom that makes a person proud, arrogant, and puffed up does not come from God. James is explicit about its origin:
But if ye have bitter envying and strife in your hearts, glory not, and lie not against the truth. This wisdom descendeth not from above, but is earthly, sensual,

devilish. For where envying and strife is, there is confusion and every evil work.

— James 3:14-16 (KJV)

In contrast, the wisdom from above is marked by humility and grace:

But the wisdom that is from above is first pure, then peaceable, gentle, and easy to be entreated, full of mercy and good fruits, without partiality, and without hypocrisy. **— James 3:17 (KJV)**

True wisdom is humble, peaceable, and easy to be entreated meaning it is open to the suggestions of others and does not insist on "my way or the highway." After stripping away the pride of minding high things and the arrogance of being wise in our own conceits, we are finally ready to embrace the central, positive command of our text.

The Heart of Meekness: "Condescend to Men of Low Estate"

After we have torn down these two worldly impulse, we arrive at the active, practical application of true meekness. This is not a suggestion but a direct command from God: "*condescend to men of low estate.*" God expects us, as His children, to actively engage with, associate with, and embrace those whom society considers lowly or ordinary.

The word "condescend" can carry a negative connotation in modern English, but its biblical meaning is beautiful. It is not about patronizing someone, but about willingly lowering oneself to be with them as an equal. Various Bible translations help capture its full meaning:

- "Be willing to associate with people of low position."
- "Be happy to be with poor people."
- "Don't be too proud to enjoy the company of ordinary people."
- "Embrace common people and ordinary tasks."
- "Make friends with nobodies."

This command challenges us at a practical level. Do you feel you are too important to vacuum the church or pick up a piece of trash on the floor? Do you only greet the "spectacular" neighbors in your apartment complex while ignoring the others? Do you come to church and only seek out the people you deem important, having no time for the "ordinary" members? If we only feel humble toward the rich and powerful but cannot be humble before those below us, we are not truly humble. We fail to understand the heart of God. But *why* would God issue such a counter-cultural command? The answer reveals a hidden, divine strategy that can unlock our own destiny.

The Hidden Power in Humility: Why We Must Condescend

God's command to condescend is not merely a test of our character; it is a revelation of His divine strategy. God often hides our greatest blessings, our most significant connections, and our "destiny helpers" in the very people society overlooks. By embracing the lowly, we align ourselves with God's method of operation and position ourselves to receive what He has for us.

A powerful example of this principle is found in the story of David's mighty men. These legendary warriors, whose accomplishments are recorded in Scripture, did not first appear to David as polished heroes. On the contrary, when they first came to him, they were outcasts.

"David therefore departed thence, and escaped to the cave Adullam: and when his brethren and all his father's house heard it, they went down thither to him. And every one that was in distress, and every one that was in debt, and every one that was discontented,

gathered themselves unto him; and he became a captain over them: and there were with him about four hundred men." — **1 Samuel 22:1-2 (KJV)**

The men who would become David's greatest assets were initially "in distress," "in debt," and "discontented." They were men of low estate. Your destiny helpers may not arrive wearing Gucci and Louis Vuitton. The CEO you will need to approach tomorrow, God may bring before you today as an ordinary person you can befriend with the simple gift of an ice cream.

The Apostle Paul provides the ultimate theological reason for this divine principle in his letter to the Corinthians. He explains that God has deliberately chosen to work through the humble and the overlooked to accomplish His purposes.

"For ye see your calling, brethren, how that not many wise men after the flesh, not many mighty, not many noble, are called: But God hath chosen the foolish things of the world to confound the wise; and God hath chosen the weak things of the world to confound the things which are mighty; And base things of the world, and things which are despised, hath God chosen, yea, and things which are not, to bring to nought things that are: That no flesh should glory in his presence." — **1 Corinthians 1:26-29 (KJV)**

God's plan is to use the "foolish," the "weak," the "base," and the "despised" to achieve His will. He does this for a specific reason: so that no human being can boast in His presence. The wise and mighty people you long to connect with today may be standing right in front of you, hidden in the form of the weak and the foolish. Therefore, embracing the lowly is not just an act of charity; it is a profound act of faith in God's hidden wisdom and sovereign power.

Conclusion: A Change of Heart and Eyes

As I reflect on this journey, I see a clear path God has laid out for us. It begins with rejecting the world's false system of class and status. It continues inward, as we must repent of the high-mindedness that makes us chase after prestige and the intellectual pride that convinces us we are wise in our own conceits.

Finally, it calls us to action—to obey the divine command to willingly and joyfully condescend to men of low estate, enjoying the company of ordinary people and embracing common tasks. We do this not only because it is right, but because we trust that God has hidden His greatest treasures in the most humble of vessels. Let this understanding lead us to a change of both heart and eyes.

CHAPTER FOUR

Blessed Are The Meek

AS WE ARRIVE AT THIS FINAL CHAPTER, we turn our attention to the blessedness of this mighty virtue of meekness. But before we can get to the blessedness of meekness, we must first grasp a critical, foundational principle. True, biblical meekness requires that we first sanctify the Lord God in our hearts. This chapter, therefore, will be divided into two distinct halves. First, we will examine what it truly means to sanctify God—to set Him apart and give Him the glory He alone is due. Then, in the second half, we will explore the profound and specific blessings that God promises to pour out upon those who walk in the power of a meek and humble spirit.

Part 1: Sanctifying the Lord

The Command to Sanctify God

The principle of sanctifying God is not merely a gentle suggestion; it is a divine command that underpins the entire practice of meekness. How we respond when God works through us, especially when He uses us to accomplish extraordinary things, becomes a critical test of our hearts. It is in these moments of divine enablement that our character is revealed. Are we quick to take a bow and accept the applause, or do we intentionally deflect the praise to the one true source of all power?

The Apostle Peter gives us a direct command that connects this vital act of sanctification with the posture of meekness. In his first epistle, Peter instructs believers on how to respond to those who question their faith:

"...and if ye suffer for righteousness sake, happy are ye: and be not afraid of their terror, neither be troubled; But sanctify the Lord God in your hearts: and be ready always to give an answer to every man that asketh you a reason of the hope that is in you with meekness and fear." — **1 Peter 3:14-15 (KJV)**

Notice the direct link: the instruction to give an answer "with meekness and fear" is the outflow of a heart that has first sanctified the Lord God. This means we must not answer as if we "know it all" or carry an air of superiority. Even when you are talking to sinners and those that are living some way, you can have a way of feeling that you are better. But God said even to them, we should not feel that way. We are commanded to respond from a place of humility, recognizing that any wisdom or hope we possess is a gift from God, not a product of our own merit. To fully comprehend the gravity of this command, we must examine the story of a great leader who failed at this very point—with devastating and permanent consequences.

A Costly Mistake: The Case of Moses

The failure of Moses to sanctify God in a critical moment cost him entry into the promised land. This story illustrates with sobering clarity that failing to give God His due glory is a serious error and a serious crime in His eyes, especially for those whom He uses mightily. God's final judgment on Moses is recorded in Deuteronomy, where He explains precisely why this beloved leader would not cross the Jordan River:

"Because ye trespassed against me among the children of Israel at the waters of MeribahKadesh, in the wilderness of Zin; because ye sanctified me not in the midst of the children of Israel. Yet thou shalt see the land before thee; but thou shalt not go thither unto the land which I give the children of Israel."

— **Deuteronomy 32:51-52 (KJV)**

To understand this judgment, we must return to the incident recorded in the book of Numbers. The children of Israel were in the wilderness, thirsty and complaining against Moses. In response, Moses sought the Lord, who gave him a very clear and specific instruction:

Take the rod, and gather thou the assembly together, thou, and Aaron thy brother, and speak ye unto the rock before their eyes; and it shall give forth his water, and thou shalt bring forth to them water out of the rock: so thou shalt give the congregation and their beasts drink. — **Numbers 20:8 (KJV)**

However, filled with frustration and anger, Moses disobeyed. Instead of speaking to the rock, he addressed the people with contempt and took credit for the miracle that was about to occur. He shouted:

...Hear now, ye rebels; must we fetch you water out of this rock? — **Numbers 20:10 (KJV)**

Then, as Scripture records, he "smote the rock twice" with his rod, and water came forth abundantly. And here is a powerful point you must understand: the miracle happened even in disobedience. That's why if somebody performs a miracle, it doesn't mean he's right with God. The people drank and were satisfied, but God was not. In the very moment the miracle was unfolding, God delivered His rebuke:

Because ye believed me not, to sanctify me in the eyes of the children of Israel, therefore ye shall not bring this congregation into the land which I have given them. — **Numbers 20:12 (KJV)**

The core of Moses's error was his failure to make a clear distinction between the human vessel and the divine source of power. The fallen nature of man has a way of glorifying the vessel God used more than the God who used the vessel. God had instructed Moses simply to *speak* to the rock so that the people would know that the miracle was not a result of Moses or his famous rod, but of God's supernatural power alone. Instead, Moses's angry words ("ye rebels") and his possessive question ("must **we** fetch you water?") glorified the man instead of God.

This story teaches us a vital lesson. Right now, God may not be using you mightily. You can say "must we," and God will clap for you; He will not punish you because everybody knows you are a human being. But when you start doing things that human beings can't do, at that time, this error is a serious error.

While Moses provides a cautionary tale, Scripture also gives us powerful examples of leaders who understood this principle and modeled it perfectly.

Examples of True Sanctification

In stark contrast to the tragic failure of Moses, we can learn how to properly sanctify God by examining the actions of others who faced similar moments of public recognition and miraculous power.

Paul and Barnabas: Deflecting Worship

In the city of Lystra, the Apostle Paul performed a remarkable miracle. Seeing a man who had been crippled from birth, Paul perceived that he had faith to be healed and commanded him with a loud voice: "...*Stand upright on thy feet*" (Acts 14:10).
Immediately, the man leaped up and began to walk. The crowd was stunned. In their pagan worldview, they could only conclude one thing: "*the gods are come down to us in the likeness of men*" (Acts 14:11). They

began preparing to offer sacrifices to Paul and his companion, Barnabas.

Their response was immediate, dramatic, and decisive. The Bible says they "*rent their clothes, and ran in among the people, crying out*" (Acts 14:14). This was not a calm refusal; it was a visceral reaction of horror. I know if it was some of us today, I wouldn't rent my clothes. I'd just walk majestically with my guys and say, "Oh, don't do that. Don't." That's how I would have spoken. But Paul didn't do that. Their words provide a perfect model of what it means to sanctify the Lord:

...Sirs, why do ye these things? We also are men of like passions with you, and preach unto you that ye should turn from these vanities unto the living God.

— Acts 14:15 (KJV)

In that critical moment, they immediately made the distinction. They drew a clear line between themselves—men with "like passions" like the idolaters they were speaking to—and the living God who was the true source of all power.

Daniel: Ascribing All Wisdom to God

Let me give you probably one more, then we will go to the blessedness. Daniel provides another flawless example. Brought before King Nebuchadnezzar, he faced an impossible task: reveal both a dream and its interpretation, a feat all other wise men declared only "the gods" could accomplish. When Daniel was brought in, he first acknowledged the limits of human ability:

Daniel answered in the presence of the king, and said, The secret which the king hath demanded cannot the wise men, the astrologers, the magicians, the sooth-sayers, shew unto the king

— **Daniel 2:27 (KJV)**

Having established that no man on earth could fulfill the king's request, Daniel immediately deflected all attention and glory away from himself and toward God:

But there is a God in heaven that revealeth secrets, and maketh known to the king Nebuchadnezzar what shall be in the latter days... — **Daniel 2:28 (KJV)**

He then went a step further, making a heartfelt statement of personal humility to ensure there was absolutely no confusion about where the wisdom originated:

But as for me, this secret is not revealed to me for any wisdom that I have more than any living...

— **Daniel 2:30 (KJV)**

Daniel's response is the essence of sanctifying God. When people start crediting you with something no one else can do, the proper response is to deflect the glory. It is to make it abundantly clear that you are not special, but that the God you serve is the one revealing the secret and demonstrating the power.

The Danger of Accepting Glory

If Moses offers a solemn warning and Paul and Daniel provide a positive model, the story of King Herod reveals the severe and immediate danger of accepting praise that belongs only to God.

The book of Acts records that Herod, dressed in royal apparel, delivered a powerful oration to the people. Awed by his speech, the crowd began to shout: *"It is the voice of a god, and not of a man."* (Acts 12:22)

Unlike Paul, who tore his clothes in horror, Herod basked in the glory. He was like, shaking his head, *Yeah. What are my ratings?* And they were telling him, *Wow, you are almost at 100%.* And as he was basking in that glory, the angel of the Lord didn't even waste time. Scripture states that *"immediately the angel of the Lord smote him, because he gave not God the glory: and he was eaten of worms, and gave up the ghost"* (Acts 12:23).

The contrast is sharp and instructive. Paul and Barnabas knew this was a terrible thing and deflected the praise. Herod, however, welcomed it and faced a dreadful end. This reinforces that taking the glory due to God is a truly serious issue.

Now that we have established the critical duty of sanctifying God as a foundational act of meekness, let us turn our attention to the incredible blessings and rewards that God promises to those who faithfully walk in this powerful virtue.

Part 2: The Fivefold Blessing of the Meek

In our modern culture, meekness is often mistaken for weakness. The world champions those who brag about themselves. But in the economy of God's kingdom, meekness is not a liability; it is a superpower. It is a powerful virtue that unlocks at least five specific and profound blessings from the hand of God Himself.

Blessing #1: Inheritance of the Earth

The first and most foundational promise to the meek is one of immense scope and significance. Jesus declared it plainly in the Beatitudes: *"Blessed are the meek: for they shall inherit the earth"* (Matthew 5:5).

This is not just a spiritual platitude. The psalmist echoes this theme, recording God's invitation to ask for a global inheritance:

Ask of me, and I shall give thee the heathen for thine inheritance, and the uttermost parts of the earth for thy posse-ssion. — **Psalm 2:8 (KJV)**

The prophet Isaiah connects this inheritance directly to a meek and humble character. He describes the one to whom God gives the "desolate heritages" as *"him whom man despiseth...a servant of rulers"* (Isaiah 49:7-8). God is actively looking for meek people to whom He can entrust earthly influence and inheritance. Why? Because He doesn't want somebody who will inherit it and start taking all the credit, saying, "I'm self-made." God looks for people who can say, "It's God that helped me o." That's the Nigerian way of saying it. You have to add the "o". We all must learn to credit God for all we have. Let statements like that be sweet in our mouth.

Blessing #2: Ever-Increasing Grace and Favor

Meekness is the key that unlocks the storerooms of God's grace, giving us access not just to grace, but to *more* grace. The Bible makes a clear distinction between how God deals with the proud and the humble: *"God resisteth the proud, but giveth grace unto the humble"* (James 4:6).

We see this perfectly illustrated in the life of the young Jesus. At just twelve years old, He was in the temple, astonishing the learned doctors with His wisdom. When His worried parents found Him, He spoke of being about His "Father's business" (Luke 2:46-49).

Yet, what happened next is the crucial part. Despite His divine wisdom and the public acclaim, Jesus humbled himself. He went home with his parents and *"was subject unto them"* (Luke 2:51). And what was the direct result of this profound act of meekness? *"And Jesus increased in wisdom and stature, and in favour with God and man."* — **Luke 2:52 (KJV)**

The lesson is unmistakable. When God promotes us, when we start getting small money—you know the young ones, you start getting small money, now you think you can talk back to your mother, you think you have arrived but you have not even started paying rent. When God blesses you and you start getting something, to keep being blessed, follow the example of Jesus. He submitted to the authorities God placed in his life, and he increased in favor not only with God, but with man.

Blessing #3: Access to Divine Wisdom

There is an inseparable link between divine wisdom and a humble heart. In the book of Proverbs, wisdom is personified, and it declares its own nature and associations:

I wisdom dwell with prudence, and find out knowledge of witty inventions. The fear of the Lord is to hate evil: pride, and arrogancy, and the evil way, and the froward mouth, do I hate.

— Proverbs 8:12-13 (KJV)

Wisdom is speaking. It says, "I hate pride and arrogancy." Now, imagine this: If you really hate somebody, and you see that person coming through a particular door, you will immediately divert to another door. Wisdom says, "I hate arrogancy." So if wisdom sees an arrogant person, that's what wisdom does to that person. If you are proud, wisdom will not come to your house. It cannot dwell there.

Conversely, God makes a specific promise to guide and teach those who approach Him with a meek spirit: *The meek will he guide in judgment: and the meek will he teach his way.* — **Psalm 25:9 (KJV)**

In a world filled with so much confusion, where the blind are leading the blind, we desperately need God's guidance. This divine guidance is not available to everyone; it is a precious blessing reserved specifically for the meek.

Blessing #4: The Path to True Greatness

The world has its own definition of greatness, but God has His own way and path to greatness. When His disciples asked Him, *"Who is the greatest in the kingdom of heaven?"* (Matthew 18:1), Jesus's answer turned their worldview upside down. He called over a little child and declared:

Whosoever therefore shall humble himself as this little child, the same is greatest in the kingdom of heaven.

— Matthew 18:4 (KJV)

In God's kingdom, our greatness is not measured by our accomplishments but by our capacity for humility. The ultimate biblical example of this is Moses. Scripture describes his unparalleled status: *"And there arose not a prophet since in Israel like unto Moses...in all the signs and the wonders which the Lord sent him to do...and in all that mighty hand, and in all that great terror which Moses shewed in the sight of all Israel"* (Deuteronomy 34:10-12). But what was the foundation of this unparalleled greatness?

"Now the man Moses was very meek, above all the men which were upon the face of the earth."

— Numbers 12:3 (KJV)

His extraordinary anointing was built on a foundation of extraordinary humility. If we truly desire to be great, we have to be competing for the most humble person. That's where the competition is. You think you are humble? Oh, you've not seen anything! Then you humble yourself more. That's a better competition. Anyone that can humble himself, that's God's way to the top.

Blessing #5: Rest and Salvation for the Soul

Finally, meekness is the pathway to finding true peace for our souls. In a world that leaves us weary and burdened, Jesus offers a profound invitation and a clear solution:

Come unto me, all ye that labour and are heavy laden, and I will give you rest. Take my yoke upon you, and learn of me; for I am meek and lowly in heart, and ye shall find rest unto your souls.

— Matthew 11:28-29 (KJV)

Of all the things we could learn from Jesus, He highlights one virtue above all others as the key to finding rest: His meekness. If you want to find rest, the thing you should be learning from Him is His meekness. Pride is exhausting; it forces us to strive and defend ourselves. Meekness allows us to rest in God's care, and this rest is part of the salvation with which God adorns the lives of the humble. As the psalmist beautifully declares:

For the Lord taketh pleasure in his people: he will beautify the meek with salvation.

— Psalm 149:4 (KJV)

Meekness is not a dull or burdensome duty. It is a beautiful path that leads to rest for our souls, guidance for our steps, ever-increasing favor, and a greatness that is recognized in heaven. It is a virtue so precious to God that He Himself promises to take pleasure in the meek and to beautify their lives with all the blessings of His complete salvation. May we all embrace this powerful virtue and allow God to manifest His strength through our humility.

***

A Study Guide

Short Answer Quiz

Instructions: Answer the following questions in two to three sentences each

1. What are the three facets that form the biblical foundation of meekness?

2. Explain the universal spiritual law of "the way up is down" as described in the text.

3. What is the biblical definition of being "under the mighty hand of God"?

4. According to the author, how is the sin of "respect of persons" different from the command to honor those in authority?

5. What are the two prohibitions given in Romans 12:16 that must be overcome to develop a meek spirit?

6. Explain why God's command to "condescend to men of low estate" is described as a divine strategy.

7. What does it mean to "sanctify the Lord God in your hearts"?

8. Describe the costly mistake made by Moses at the waters of Meribah-Kadesh and its consequence.

9. According to the text, what is the primary difference between worldly wisdom and the wisdom that comes from God?

10. List and briefly explain two of the five specific blessings promised to the meek.

***

Answer Key

1. The three facets of biblical meekness are
    spiritual "poverty," humility, and being "small
    in your own eyes." Spiritual "poverty" refers to
    a state of total dependence on God, not a lack
    of material wealth. Humility is a lowly heart, an
    inward state modeled by Jesus, while being
    "small in your own eyes" is the outward
    expression of refusing to see oneself as
    important in God's presence.

2. The universal spiritual law of "the way up is
    down" states that those who exalt themselves
    will be brought low, while those who humble
    themselves will be exalted by God. This
    principle is illustrated by the contrast between
    Satan's downfall through pride and Christ's
    exaltation through humility. It requires a
    person to actively choose to humble
    themselves, which is distinct from humiliation,
    which occurs when God has to bring a self-
    exalted person down.

3. To be "under the mighty hand of God" is a
    command to place oneself "under the authority
    of God." The text defines this by referencing

Jeremiah 27, where being "in the hand of" King Nebuchadnezzar meant being "under the authority of" him. Since all authority has been given to Jesus, this means submitting to the legitimate, delegated authorities He has established on earth.

4. The sin of "respect of persons" is treating people differently based on their wealth, appearance, or social class, which James condemns as being driven by "evil thoughts." Honoring authority, by contrast, is a biblical command to honor the God-given *positions* people hold, such as a church leader or government official, regardless of their personal wealth or status. The former is based on worldly advantage, while the latter is based on God's ordained structure.

5. The two prohibitions are to "mind not high things" and "be not wise in your own conceits." Minding high things refers to being "high-minded" or haughty, fixating on status and associating only with the elite. Being wise in your own conceits is an internal, intellectual pride that convinces a person they are smarter

than everyone else and that their opinions are superior.

6. The command to condescend is a divine strategy because God often hides a person's greatest blessings and "destiny helpers" in the very people society overlooks. The text uses the example of David, whose mighty men first came to him as a group of outcasts who were in debt, distress, and discontented. By embracing the lowly, believers align with God's method of using the "weak" and "despised" to accomplish His will so that no human can boast.

7. To "sanctify the Lord God in your hearts" is the foundational act of meekness, meaning to set God apart and intentionally give Him the glory He alone is due. It involves making a clear distinction between the human vessel God uses and the divine source of power, especially in moments of miraculous works or public recognition. It means deflecting praise from oneself to God, as exemplified by Daniel and the apostles Paul and Barnabas.

8. At Meribah-Kadesh, Moses was instructed by God to speak to a rock to bring forth water, but in anger, he struck the rock twice. More

importantly, he failed to sanctify God by saying, "must *we* fetch you water out of this rock?", taking partial credit for the miracle. Because he did not give God the proper glory, God barred him from entering the Promised Land.

9. Worldly wisdom is described as "earthly, sensual, devilish," and is characterized by bitter envying, strife, pride, and arrogance. The wisdom that comes from God, in contrast, is identified by its "meekness." Heavenly wisdom is described as pure, peaceable, gentle, full of mercy, and "easy to be entreated," meaning it is open to the suggestions of others.

10. Two of the five blessings are the **Inheritance of the Earth** and **Access to Divine Wisdom**. Jesus promised in the Beatitudes that the meek would inherit the earth, meaning God entrusts them with earthly influence. The text also states that God reserves divine guidance for the meek ("The meek will he guide in judgment") because wisdom itself hates pride and arrogance and will not associate with a proud person.

***

Essay Questions

1. Using the examples of King David, Jesus, and the Apostle Paul, elaborate on the three facets of biblical meekness: spiritual "poverty," humility, and being "small in your own eyes."

2. Compare and contrast the paths of Lucifer and King Uzziah with the path of Jesus Christ. How do their stories illustrate the "universal spiritual law" that self-exaltation leads to being brought low, while humility leads to exaltation?

3. The source argues that humbling oneself "under the mighty hand of God" is a series of practical, daily actions. Define this concept and then describe in detail the six spheres of delegated authority where believers are commanded to demonstrate submission.

4. Analyze the world's system of social stratification as presented in the text. How does the command to "condescend to men of low estate," coupled with the prohibitions against being "high-minded" and "wise in your own conceits," directly challenge this worldly system?

5. Explain why "sanctifying the Lord God" is presented as the foundational act of meekness. Use the contrasting biblical examples of Moses, Daniel, Paul and Barnabas, and King Herod to illustrate both the severe consequences of failing this test and the proper way to give God glory.

***

Glossary of Key Terms

Term	Definition
Condescend	To willingly lower oneself to associate with people of a lower position as an equal. It involves enjoying the company of ordinary people and embracing common tasks, rather than patronizing them.
Delegated Authorities	The legitimate structures of authority on earth established by God, which are extensions of the ultimate authority of Jesus Christ. The text identifies six spheres: government, employers, husbands (in marriage), parents, church elders, and fellow believers (in mutual submission).
Destiny Helpers	Significant people God brings into a person's life to help them fulfill their purpose. The author argues these individuals are often hidden in the "men of low estate" whom society overlooks.

Exousia	The Greek word for "power" used in Matthew 28:18, which specifically means authority.
Fake Submission	The act of claiming to humbly submit to God's unseen authority while actively disrespecting, dishonoring, and resisting the visible, delegated authorities He has established on earth.
High-Minded	A state of being haughty, or "bluntantly and disdainfully proud." It is an attitude of superiority and contempt for people or things perceived to be inferior, and it manifests in fixating on status, prestige, and association with the elite.
Humiliation	The state of being brought low by God as a consequence of having first exalted oneself. It is distinct from humility, which is a voluntary choice to humble oneself.
Humility	The second facet of meekness, defined as an inward state of having a "lowly

	heart." It is a genuine, internal posture modeled by Jesus Christ.
Meekness	A mighty spiritual virtue, often misunderstood as weakness, that is an indispensable quality for believers. Its biblical foundation consists of three facets: spiritual "poverty" (dependence on God), humility (a lowly heart), and being "small in your own eyes."
Pride	The lethal counterfeit to meekness, which leads down the path of self-exaltation. It is identified as "the condemnation of the devil" and was the cause of Lucifer's fall from heaven.
Respect of Persons	The sin of treating people differently based on their worldly advantages, such as wealth, social status, or appearance. This practice is condemned in Scripture as being partial and driven by "evil thoughts."
Sanctify the Lord God	The foundational act of meekness; to set God apart by intentionally and publicly giving Him the glory He is due, especially after He has performed

	a mighty work through a person. It involves deflecting praise from the human vessel to the divine source.
Self-Exaltation	The act of trying to lift oneself up, which is a spiritually lethal path that stands in direct opposition to God's will. It is the core of pride and always ends in being brought low.
Spiritual "Poverty"	The first facet of meekness, describing a state of the heart that is in total dependence on God. It is a deep, internal acknowledgment that one can do nothing of true spiritual value on their own.
Under the Mighty Hand of God	A biblical phrase meaning to be "under the authority of God." This is not a mystical feeling but a practical command to submit to the delegated authorities God has placed in one's life.
Universal Spiritual Law	The principle that "the way up is down." It is a spiritual certainty that whoever exalts himself will be abased (brought low), and whoever humbles himself will be exalted.

Wise in Your Own Conceits	An internal dimension of pride; the arrogance that convinces a person they are smarter than others, that their opinions are superior, and that their contributions are always the most valuable.

About the Author

Pastor Joshua Asiedu, originally a Ghanaian, was born in Nigeria and raised as a PK. In 2007 moved to United States where he received his call into full time ministry. He Earned his Bachelor of Arts Degree in Theological Studies at the University of Valley Forge, Phoenixville PA. He has served in the local church in various capacities including as an associate And resident pastor.

He is currently the Senior Pastor at Lifegate Assembly of God Arlington Texas. A gifted teacher of the Word with a passion to see God's people equipped with the knowledge of the truth that is after godliness. Lives in Texas with his amazing wife Shiro and their beautiful daughter.

Thanks for reading! Please add a short review on Amazon and let me know what you thought!

Follow Us On YouTube:
Lifegate Broadcast

www.ingramcontent.com/pod-product-compliance
Lightning Source LLC
Chambersburg PA
CBHW020413150626
46554CB00013B/947